BIRD TALK

by
Lenore Keeshig-Tobias
illustrated by
Irving Toddy

HARCOURT BRACE & COMPANY
Orlando Atlanta Austin Boston San Francisco Chicago Dallas New York
Toronto London

Illustrations by Irving Toddy
Illustrations copyright © 1994 by Harcourt Brace & Company

This edition is published by special arrangement with Sister Vision.

Grateful acknowledgment is made to Sister Vision: Black Women and
Women of Colour Press, Toronto, Ontario, Canada, for permission to reprint
Bird Talk by Lenore Keeshig-Tobias. Text copyright © 1991 by Lenore
Keeshig-Tobias. English translation copyright © 1991 by Shirley Pheasant
Williams.

Printed in Mexico

ISBN 0-15-302146-2

3 4 5 6 7 8 9 10   050   97 96 95 94

BIRD TALK

by
Lenore Keeshig-Tobias
illustrated by
Irving Toddy

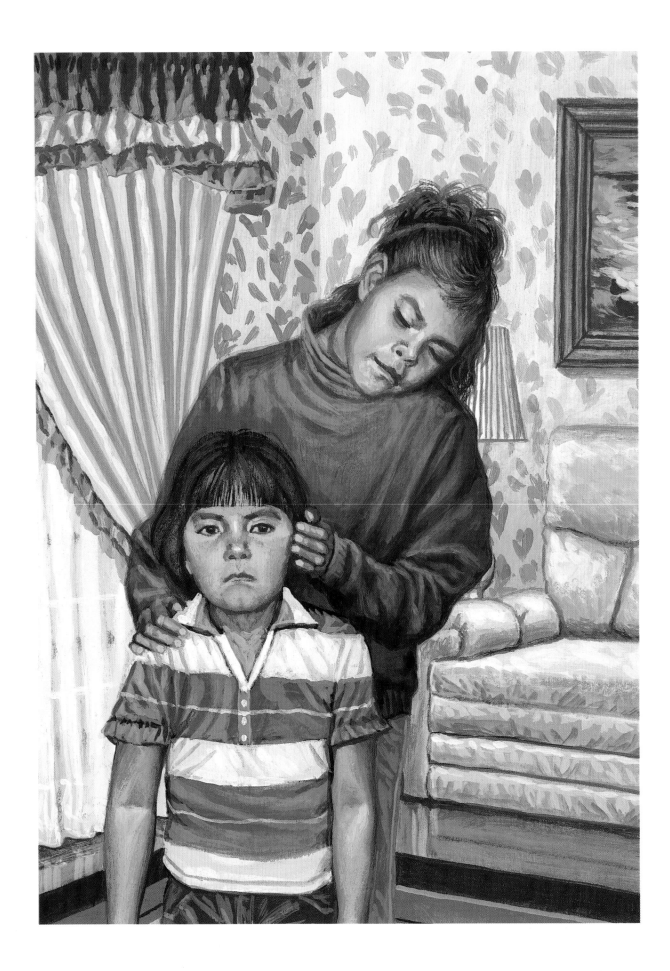

Polly had a bad day. I could tell. She was very, very quiet after school. I thought she was sick and put my hand on her face. "Leave me alone," she said.

"What's the matter?" I said.

"Nothing," she said.

When we got home, Polly went to the bedroom and stayed there. All afternoon. She didn't want to go down to the playground. She didn't want to help with dinner. She didn't want to lick the mixing bowl clean. All she wanted to do was look at our family picture album.

My Momma Brown Bird had a good day. I could
tell. She was baking a chocolate cake. Mmm. She always
makes a special treat for me and my sister, Polly, when she
has a good day. And she had one. I could smell it.

I had a good day too. I painted a real nice picture of a crow. And I wrote a story to go with it. Uncle Bob told the story to me long ago, before Polly and Momma and I moved to the city. Teacher said it was good work. And my school friends thought it was cool.

After dinner, I was doing my homework. I could
hear Polly on the balcony calling to the birds, "Hello,
brown birds. Hello. Nobody asks you where *your*
feathers are."

Momma called out to Polly, "Well, Brown Baby
Bird, what did you do in school today?"

Polly is Momma's Brown Baby Bird because she is the youngest. Momma calls me "Brown Bird." I guess it's like when other mothers call their kids "honey" or "sweetie." I like "Brown Bird." It makes me feel good and it makes brown special.

Well, Momma called out to Polly again, "Polly, what did you do in school today?"

"Oh, nothing," answered Polly. That was strange. Polly always had something to talk about.

"You had a bad day?" Momma asked.

My little sister didn't answer. She came in and sat
on the couch. I heard it squeak. "You had a bad day?"
Momma asked again, more softly this time.

Finally, after a long while Polly said, "Yes... I
mean no." And then she said, "Momma, I don't feel like
an Indian."

I sat up straight. Nokmis and Mishomis told us always to be proud of who we are, especially when we're away from home.

"Why don't you feel like an Indian, Polly?" Momma asked.

"Because I don't know much about Indian things," answered Polly. "I don't even think I look like an Indian girl."

Polly sounded so sad. I left my homework and
went to sit with Momma and her. Polly used to be a
happy little girl all the time, except when she got into
mischief, of course. After we moved to the city, she
would get real lonesome sometimes.

Momma and I waited until Polly was ready to talk. And then it all poured out. Polly missed Nokmis and Mishomis. (That's Gramma and Grampa in our language.) She missed our aunties and uncles and cousins. (We have a very big, big family.) She missed Uncle Bob's hunting dog, Rocky. She missed the house we used to live in. Momma and I missed those things too. But Momma was in college now, so we had to be in the city.

"At recess," continued Polly, "some kids wanted to play cowboys and Indians. And I said it was not a nice game. Tommy said, 'How do you know?' I said, 'I know because I'm Indian.' Tommy said, 'Oh yeah, where's your feathers then?' And then Jasmine said, 'If you're Indian why don't you come from India?' And Maria said I looked like Snow White because my skin was not red."

Polly closed her eyes tight and squeezed two big tears out. Momma gave her some tissues. "And you didn't know what to say?" she asked. Polly nodded. Momma put her arms around Polly and cuddled her. I put my arms around Momma and waited. I wondered what she would say.

"Do you remember the last visit home?" she asked. Momma always calls the reserve "home." Polly and I nodded our heads. Mishomis was tying language together that time.

"Tying language together" means "interpreting,"
or "translating." I love to hear him tie up the language
and untie it. He takes words from our language, makes
them into smaller words, and then tells what each word
means in English.

Like *sheebsheeb-akik*. Mishomis said most people would just say "kettle." But it really means "duck pail." That's funny, eh? *Sheebsheeb* is "duck." And *akik* is "pail." Mishomis said the old people thought a kettle looked like a duck.

Anyhow, Polly and I remembered. Mishomis was
tying English words to *Anishinabe*. I can't remember
exactly what he said. But the way Mishomis tied things, it
turned out to be "good of the earth." Then he made us
laugh when he said "good earthling." Uncle Bob was
there and made us laugh more. He made funny noises like
a flying saucer and said, "Take me to your leader."

Momma then told us about Christopher Columbus. She said there are two stories about how he named the Indians. One is that he called the people *Indeo*, which means "in God" in his language. He thought they were in the image of God. The other story is that he called the people "Indians" because he thought he had landed in India.

Momma said all people have their own names for themselves in their own language. And maybe they all mean "good of the earth." And maybe people all over the world should learn each other's names.

As for cowboys and Indians, Momma said she would talk to Polly's teacher. And maybe she would go to Polly's class and talk about Columbus. And show the kids pictures of modern-day Indians. (Momma doesn't like to say "Indians." She likes to say "Native" or "In-di-gen-ous" or "A-bo-ri-gin-al.")

After that long talk, Momma took her brown birds out to the plaza for an ice cream. Polly's was strawberry. Momma had vanilla. Mine was chocolate. Polly said mine was squashed-up-brown-worm ice cream. She was feeling better.

The weather was nice. There were lots of people in that plaza. I could hear them talking in different languages. I thought it was like waking up in the early morning, before rush hour. You can hear all the different birds singing their own bird songs in their own bird language. Sparrow, robin, wren, chickadee, and gull. They are all telling their bird children about their own bird life.

Polly and I hopped beside our bird mother. We hopped back to our bird apartment building. And into our nest of blankets and toys.

Momma came to tuck us in and turn out the light. She winked at me and said to Polly, "Well, Snow White, when summer comes, maybe you will be nice and brown."

Polly giggled and said, "Oh, I forgot..." She went to the window and said good night to the birds. Then she snuggled up to me. She whispered that she could hear little birds all over the world saying good night to their bird mothers.